Wild Plums

Barbara Conrad

FUTURECYCLE PRESS
Mineral Bluff, Georgia

Published by FutureCycle Press
Mineral Bluff, Georgia, USA

ISBN 978-1-938853-10-4

Contents

To Katy and Caroline,
who grace so many of these poems—and my life

I

...Whistle
For me, grow green for me and, as you whistle and grow green
Intangible arrows quiver and stick in the skin
And I taste at the root of the tongue the unreal of what is real.

—Wallace Stevens
Holiday in Reality

Bodegónes

17th-century Spanish genre scenes
immortalized by Velázquez, often set in taverns
or kitchens where cast iron pots on rough walls
were depicted as more significant than people

This woman frying eggs under a wide brush
of the artist's spell is not my mother, is she? Her raw
cracked hands, hard gaze at the child.

It might be any child—though isn't there more
than luminescent yolks between them?

What about the light the artist brings—to an unglazed
pot, tender skin of red onion on a crude table,
an unbroken eggshell. Such a plain life suspended
as if in meditation. As if lard from the pot

will never spatter onto a wide plank floor,
or the woman slip on a spill and shatter her bones.

In this scene, the husband-figure,
the father, will not bring home his bowery breath
or slump at the sink to swig a final jigger of bane
before she falls. He'll not stagger to her side

suddenly sober and sympathetic, or lift her
in a way I never saw him lift her.

This is where Velázquez fails me, all his glimmer
spent on brass, and that one odd shadow
of knife in an empty bowl.

Clutter Dreams

An old farm house, cracked plaster, tangled
halls of faceless knickknacks,
      your raw hands dipping and squeezing
and dipping a worn rag into ammonia and Ajax.
He is never present, your old lover.
The dream knows this is not about longing
though your dead relatives
are gathered in the kitchen in swirls of menthol
                and steam from boiling pots.

§

Gathered in the kitchen in swirls of steam,
their voices are a thin muffle.
They don't see you wrestling with years
of stubborn grime, scrubbing walls and baseboards.
      What you'd give for a different dream.
A house emptied,
just you and the dust motes.

§

Your old lover is never present.
The dream knows this is not about longing.
Or blame. Yet, the dead are gathered
      (your mother, father, Aunt Evelyn, Uncle Ern)
in the kitchen swirling in menthol
and steam from boiling pots, their voices
         a thin muffle. They don't see you
wrestling stubborn grime, cracks
and tangles. They don't see
you dipping and squeezing, bent on raw knees.

§

Ooze of yellow oil from the baseboard.
The more you scrub, the more it oozes

through plaster cracks
      and faceless knickknacks.
What you'd give for a different dream.
Your old lover, on bended knees.
               What does the dream know?
In the kitchen, a thin muffle of voices.
Dead relatives—doing what the dead do
when someone leaves the back door unlatched.

Tinted Snapshots under Glass

She reclines in a wood-slat chair
in a Florida garden, her gaze
hung like steam, every muscle slack,
my mother in her own time,
elegant slouch, her gartered legs crossed
at slender ankles, hint of bare knee
above rolled-down back seams

> *and he, no ordinary fisherman,*
> *the man in the smirk and salty cap*
> *edged on a wooden stool*
> *in a stark room of warm pastels,*
> *its door slightly ajar, my father,*
> *in a scene from Key West,*
> *man of the sea*

and she, all pearl and plum
in a cotton dress, buttoned to the neck
with fingers that may have brushed
his lips as she stepped from the tub,
pulled bobby pins from her hair,
slipped the dress on
so she could pose for him

> *in his rumpled khakis,*
> *his jaw set*
> *to spread a young man's gospel,*
> *cradling twenty pounds*
> *of grouper as he lifts his catch*
> *toward the woman*
> *behind the lens,*

woman in the hush-hush
of hibiscus and mango,

> *man in a room swarming*
> *with seaweed and fish.*

Urban Geese

Wing on wind, its hard beat
  breaking the morning silence,
   as two white billows thrust over
  the lake, onto a grassy bank.
She begins to peck at bugs and

scattered seeds. He struts and
  puffs. She puffs and flaps her feathers.
   He spreads his wingspan across
  her back, climbs on, his red wattle
nuzzling her neck. For all his quaking

he must have proclaimed himself
  the swan-god and she his Leda,
   her frowzy plumage spun
  into silky tresses by now as they wiggle
in the dewy green. These middling

yard birds won't bring forth radiance
  or conquering armies—
   only a few scrappy goslings,
  and for a minute here in the park,
a little flicker of the great myth.

The Unblooming

Spring—and multitudes
of green wet worms are wicking
their way up the willow oaks, gorging
on new shoots, scabbing the branches.

Birds too, all spin and flutter,
heavy-laden with worm-pleasure.
Here among the yet-to-bud peonies
and astilbes, one has fallen.

Scatter of fluff on the brick wall,
a slightly twisted neck.

She's a yellow-billed cuckoo, jay-sized,
white-bright, dotted with flashes of rufous
under her wings and along her long silk tail.
A shy bird, I'll come to learn,
up from South America.

So here is where the *ifs* come in.

If not for the swarm of worms, the dazzle
of green, she may have lingered in a holly
or maple sapling, laid her brood
in a saucer of twigs.

If, if, if—she had not hit the wall,
had not fallen, you would not see me

bending over this still life,
studying its perfection, and next to her,
one perfect blue-green egg,

pulsed from her body by the blow,
belly filled and emptied.

Halftones

Sun shudders toward earth.
Clouds pad the sky with old lace.
Everything about the afternoon
has gone dim gray.

I move to the edge of the cottage porch,
look out through a fringe of scrub pine,
past rail and inlet—

think of old photographs in anybody's attic.

Three stilted houses line the road here,
asbestos-weary, dull as the end of summer.
Out beyond still water,
the brown grass of an estuary.

Suddenly, as if color can no longer hold itself secret,
the shock of a catamaran's sail
slices the frame, skimming the sound.
Like a parrot in a place of gulls and gadwalls.

In a moment it passes.
Day turns back to sepia,
bone and linen film,

and I'm back to the attic—

to the untold palette of a mother's dress
on a jalousied porch in Miami, the father's necktie.
That one taken in '36. And the one in '35
of a nameless man
whose arm wraps around the mother.

What color his jacket, I wonder,
the bud in his lapel,
the cloud-studded sky.

Early on the Beach

and two brown stick-boys slicked up
in grease and rubber are wading out along the pier,
surfboards tucked under tight arms.
They look like the pilings, hard and straight.

At the water's edge a sign reads:
   No surfing within 500 yards of the pier.

On softer sand, a young couple lies
on a padded quilt, their fingers laced, if not
their tongues, as if breath depended on
their connections. They and a guitar have

spent the night. This means nothing to me,
yet something aches to tell them all
about morning gnats and wet sand wicking
through a warm blanket, about riptides

and undertows. How only yesterday I walked
this same beach, bold and salty as they are now.
That just below the ocean's smooth blue skin,
not far from the pier, there are shipwrecks.

Words from Barcelona

Hola, Mama, my daughter's first email
begins, only to be scrambled
by translation.com as *Hello Breast.*

Her sister, the one who hung like an unripe fruit
through three years of Spanish II, will get a good laugh.
Once in class she had tried to say
Monkeys come out of your butt, some cult-insult
of the nineties, but said instead
Monkeys live in your donkey.

And so it goes, the boorish no-nonsense
of language. My yellow is no one's yellow,
not gold or gamboge, ocher or buff unless
they deem it so. I choose one word and it burns.
Another filters through early dawn, settles
in a silk pigtail on a gingham pillow.

For seven months my youngest will revel
in a foreign word—a foreign world—captivated
by her own reds, blues, bursts of hill-top gold.
Flamenco, fiestas, fish baked in salt, sangria,
Sagrada Familia. I roll it on my tongue for proof.

Bar-ce-lo-na.
Then *Moth-er. Moth-er.*

Wild Plums

Look what the chill wind has brought us—
scores of cedar waxwings, filling a tamarisk tree
next to the beach cottage.

All morning they'll come and go,
forty or fifty at once, nomads in black
bandit-masks out for insects and berries.

At first we're inside watching them
gathered on the lacy branches,
some huddled near the tree's trunk, others

nodding and bobbing on the edges of twigs,
weighing down the boughs.
Their bodies are fluffed-up and full

as if the tree has suddenly sprouted
wild plums, pale yellow tinged in green,
nearly fit for picking.

We ease onto the front porch,
listen for their trill-like sounds (a small *bzeee,*
not even birdsong). Any minute

some note or gesture will signal them to dart up
and away, sweep their red-tipped wings
in synchronized twists and turns,

disappear. We can't get enough
of this frenzy. All doubt and logic aside,
this has become our morning

meditation—a cold breeze between seasons
doing whatever it does to open us up,
like turning birds into fruit.

I Kept Meaning to Tell You
about the Kingfisher at the Creek Today

The one roosting on a dead tree
by the stone bridge, first
I had ever seen, much less startled,
the way he jack-hammered
my ears with his rude stutter, banked a 180,
striping the air between us with slate-blue ribbons.

But all day there were interruptions.

Does a thought ever flutter like feathers
in your head, imagined as conversation,
its words and rhythms worked and re-worked
on your tongue until you can taste
the message in your mouth?
Images, inflections, each noun, verb,
appositive phrase crafted, their anticipated tone
mellow as an old Billie Holiday, until by mid-day
you're not sure if you've sung them or not.

Maybe the words don't matter anyway,
reality being *not* that blue clay pot
on the kitchen counter next to the crossword,
but the image of yourself molding wet mud,
your arms spattered, loose rotations of your body
as you lean into the wheel's orbit.

Can't you tell how all day today
I've seemed a little off-kilter? How at the creek
I must have seen something—a kingfisher,
for instance—lift easily from its perch,
flash me a copper eye,
circle up into its own riddle?

Re-Vamped

Being under the influence of dandelions
and other small things, I didn't know it then
but even at ten I wanted my mother bold.

Brassy sassy, drenched in spice
like her younger sister my aunt, who
that year came to live with us

wearing an Austin Healey convertible
and open-toed see-through sandals, exposing
shiny toenails red as my face

when she would coo and call me Sexy.
That year is why I now rewrite my mother
squeezing her twin bed tight

against my father's and re-shaping them
into one plump heart, prying open
their goodnight kisses, dressing her

with nouns that echo and verbs that quiver
like Jell-O, cherry-slivered, served
from a wide-mouth porcelain bowl,

white as winter flesh,
every bit of her
finally about dessert.

High Desert

for Claude

On a long stretch between Red Flint Gorge
        and Vernal, Utah, an unexpected call
comes in that the husband of a friend

has died. We'll keep crossing the country
as planned, I say, let me know how she's doing.
        Before we reach the redwoods,

I'll get an update. Memorial service
        jam-packed, she clinging limp
to the arms of their grown children,

female priest donning a red bow tie
(*his* trademark) for the eulogy,
        not a dry eye.

Along this highway, the landscape
        rises and falls. His death settles
onto rocky ridgetops and into sheltered basins.

The rutting cry of a distant elk seems
        woeful and right. And the colors—
red rock in flames,

lodgepole pines lifting to meet a sky
so blue it almost hurts to look up.
        Over the desert,

a scatter of blooms—each bud
that will become flower, that will become
        seed, that will become flower.

Paperwhites

The air in the room this morning
       is a sweet breath of new blooms,
broken at last from thin leafy-green girdles.
All week I've watched the bulbs,
          like small fists,
shift and strain in their crowded pot,
roots burrowing their way down
       among smooth stones, silver-green stems
up from a dark place
   arcing toward the window,
as if following an ancient map,
giving in to light.
          White light, white breath.

A child I once knew would often say
    before I was born, I was dead,
and we'd laugh,
         or babble some hidebound creed.
Here in this blaze of small lace trifles
        may be a new wisdom—
   each blossom resting
inside its den of nerve and tissue,
      coy as death, yet not dead.
   I think of the child
and trillions of seeds, *in absentia,* pulsing,
    waiting to shimmer—
       small flames of wild, white heat.

Sweet

One of us at the supper table
would hear it coming up the hill
and whisper *Bugman.*

Then without asking we'd push back unfinished
chicken and gravy, bolt from our chairs,

dash barefoot out the screen door
across a crooked flagstone walk
into the street

to skip and dart behind the little truck,
its engine slowly groaning
as it sowed a blue-gray fog
of sweet toxins for us to revel in.

Throughout the neighborhood—the slamming
of doors, running of children
to join our weekly mosquito-killing ritual,

eyes burning, dank smell in our hair,
the laughing, the light. All of us light,

like those storybook youngsters
in a little river town, charmed by the cane pipe
of a red-and-gold-coated gypsy,
hired to rid the village of harm with his melody.

All night the parents must have called out
for their runabouts to come back,
while in the shadows

the tug of familiar nurture
was weakening under a new weight
of delicious unknowing.

Dead Mouse in the Water Bowl

Shadow floating in the dog's dish—
spur of the cats' ruckus no doubt.
Lump of bone and gristle,
so perfect, still
in its little silk coat, belly down.

Though I guessed it was dead,
I held out 'til morning—cautiously
dumping the corpse in the toilet,
a blessing on my lips.

That other time, when she sang out
Look, Mom, Goldie's floating!
I knew for sure
the fish in the bowl had died.
Sidewise its color shimmered,
its gills no stiffer than in life.
For a bit I let her soft joy linger

before it turned cold and dropped
like a stone into the room.

Past Curfew

for Katy and her friend Julie

1:37 a.m.

You lie flat in some kind of milky way,
clock swallowing the night with its little bites,
waiting for a key
to turn off the clamp in your chest,
your head too heavy
for the feather pillow, too light
for sleep. You lie flat, knowing
that not knowing may be better.

1:48 a.m.

Dance ended at one. Something now festers
like a splinter left for days
in your thumb. You would gladly
cut it off,
thumb you rely on, sign
that sets humans apart,
the blame for this pain.

2:09 a.m.

You remember how it feels to totter
at the end of the high dive, vibration
of board slithering up through your body,
knowing if you never dive
you'll never get wet, leaning over the edge,
wanting to free fall, wondering if
you'll remember to breathe
when you hit the water.

On Buying a Writing Desk after the Death of My Daughter's Best Friend

On Buying a Writing Desk after
the Death of My Daughter's Best Friend

for Michael

When the decorator tells me
the old table I like is too big for a desk,

I tell the woman *I'll take it*
and think of the boy who couldn't be coached.

The coach said so—would watch him
blowing free in his own wind

up and down the soccer field, defiant
ringlets of hair a halo on his unleashed body.

The wood beneath my fingers is bold,
a rich heart pine the color of honey,

a good place to write these words.
I rub its shiny skin and think about the boy

bearing down on the goal, the boy too big
for the soccer field,

the school,
the gravity of this earth.

Watch this, the coach would say before a play
and—after the shot—*Did you see that?*

Snake

for Fred

Outside his doublewide, he showed
us bluebirds, snow
peas growing, tree
choked in vines he'd

fashion to a walking stick—had
to be straight, wrapped
in a sweet snake,
digging deep trails.

Saw him once again at sixty,
could not be fixed,
was coiled in tubes,
skin bluebird blue.

Alone in the Kitchen
with a Basket of Plums

Breasts wilting, her daughters now grown,
she stands stoic
against aging
reality.

Wishing she had nursed them longer,
recalling songs
that stimulate
nipples' aching

for tender sucking of soft gums.
She plucks a plum
so wet, full, ripe,
her own sweet bite.

Brownstones

Defiant, these ladies still rock,
keep idle watch
on 44th
and Pine. Flowers

languish, once caressed their arms, laps
empty now, lips
and lids have paled,
tan on pastel

chiffon withered in wrinkles from
sun, soot. While one
boasts of phony
hips, lifted bones.

Sharon Amity and Monroe

Don't bury me on this corner
with blaring horns,
plastic blooms, men
weeding out sins

ChemLawn missed. Grow weeds on my grave,
smell of skunk. Grace
me with mountain
mulch, naked in

dirt, no marker. Bed my ashes
near creeks' passes.
Follow snow on
moss to find me.

Childhood Portrait on a Bedroom Wall

The girl in the frame smirks
at you through fifty years of glass,
magazines stacked
on an old wicker basket upside down.
It's all upside down now—
whopsided will-silly whirligiggled
ig-pay-atin-lay ache-bray your mother's ack-bay—
you know your mother can't come back.

The red cat kneads your chest,
Persephone wanders her hot cave,
and no one has had enough for supper.
From a pore in the pillowcase, granny-apple-green,
a white feather pokes the scene,
an angel's wing.
A fan drones on and on.

Who made that dream catcher
on the bedpost anyway,
child with the red sled or the one who
loved bears on stairs at Christmas?
Do bears have wings or stuffed tigers live forever?
A zebra on the other wall glares back
at the girl in the glass,
cat crossing over by now, winking fluff and dust,
and you waiting
for someone to turn out the light.

II

Now the earth is spinning round me,
dizzying me,
like metal at the sound of bells.

—*Pablo Neruda*

Snorkeling the Big Island

for my daughters

How limp we're becoming
in the warm salt broth, our muscles lolling
like spent seaweed.

For a little while now, we'll not claim the constellation
beneath us. Blues, yellows and reds will dart and nibble at coral
we dare not touch,

unconscious of the colors we've assigned them
or the names—trunkfish, yelloweye tang, sabre-toothed blenny—
or dominion.

We glance back. Below us a sea turtle
lifts her great green weight off the sand.
     Nimble acrobat,

she rises to the surface, snaps a beak full of what we've come
to call our air, returns her ancient bulk downward, unfettered.
For millions of years

myths have named her. Honu. Kauila. *Great Mythical Mother.*
Always, she's carried the world on her back.
     We float until

we can float no more. Unfolding, we remake ourselves
long and awkward, crawl onto rock ledges, plod across crevices,
unmistakably evolved.

Gospel

for those in Georgia who propose
placing stickers in textbooks
stating that evolution is a theory

Tell it to the chimpanzees,
those great African apes whose DNA
is more like ours than an orangutan's
or a gorilla's. Tell it to the orangutans,
     Annabelle and Alex,
their brains spinning luminous
under tufts of wild ginger.

Gorillas and bonobos would need to know,
     Pumbu and Tam Tam.
And if you believe in the everlasting, speak
to the bones of that six-million-year-old hybrid
from Kenya, our common link.

Then quell your wrangle, sit back
and watch the world tilt, all gravity and spin,
restless fool of dirt and magma,
inexplicable enterprise.

Watch for stars to settle into black chiffon
and dare to puzzle how even a shim of moon
could be whittled into such silver.

Off-season

Calendar-perfect this autumn,
its untainted bursts of amber and rust,
a woodsy smell. But fingers
of crisp air have turned sultry and,
bathed in wet mist, grind the carpet
of dry leaves into a slippery brown paste.

See how it sticks to the soles
of our shoes, follows us in
through the back door while outside a vague
gray looks like winter, but humors us
with humidity and heat. Inside, a leftover
summer fly hunkers at a window, as if

to taunt next spring's narcissus (which by the way
are peeking from an earth that should be
freezing by now). So baffled are we by the gaps
in our weather—plans made, calendar page
switched, four seasons pure
as our birth orders. Our boxes are checked,

except for the woman who should have been
a man, man of color, god of our youth who looks like
a Hebrew but answers to Buddha, Vishnu or Light.
Except for this fall when we still walk
barefoot in slanted sunlight, and no one
can fathom the absence of frost.

Whit

On learning that a single step
at the ocean's edge,
the gravity of one foot
on matted sand, will crush
a thousand creatures, each only
a few cells wide and off-putting
when magnified—the invisible,
the unredeemed—I wonder
if I were the Buddha would I ever
step again along the shore
onto the world.

If there *is* a god
in the sky—storm- or star-studded,
does she falter in the riddle
of going out or staying in.

What I scoop into my hand
I lift in the name
of all who have no names.

So how much weight gives rise to
oblivion—sandpiper, pelican,
laughing gull, children hunkered
on bony knees—crawling
pawing   patting   mauling.

What universe lives beneath.

Would I go there, would I alter
my human pedigree for a brief life
of cool foam, a quiet rustle
of dune grass, salt from the sea.

Last Night I Found Jesus

This time he came in a gasp
like someone sucking air from a secret.
I unplugged the source, dismantled
the vacuum hose, and there he was, tangled
in a wad of cat hair and lint. Little figurine,
gazing out in blessed resignation—

lost for so many Christmases.
I held him in my palm like a wafer.
God or goddess, who could tell,
his private parts shrouded in a whittled diaper.
Had he liked his reprieve
from the barn scene? All those donkeys

and itchy hay, hubbub of angels
coming out of nowhere
like a Hallmark commercial?
For two years, a plastic teddy bear had been
his stand-in, red-vested, gold-crowned,
part of my daughter's ornament set.

So why would I find him now, stuck
in a tunnel with all my grime and clutter,
when doctrine says
he'd come in glory and light?
And who had turned *me* into *savior?*
I was testy—

then softened. Such a burden,
all my questions for a dusty baby. No wonder
he'd hidden so long behind the dresser.
Poor little image. Infant icon.
Precious, mysterious
hand-carved nugget of wood.

A Starving Musician Takes a Church Job

for Mark

Are you saved, the lead singer asked
in the interview, *and do you know why
I joined this church? Because if people
don't follow Jesus—when he comes back,
God will chop their heads off.*

He took the gig anyway,
and every Sunday morning
for two hours and four hundred dollars,
just in case they're on to something,
he beats the Hell out of the drums.

Bulldozer

Second day of demolition, 7 a.m.,
and all the parts in their places.
Copper tubing, orange cones,
long lengths of blue-sky water pipe
plastic and new, wider they say—
the men in boots and muscles.
This will be good for you.

John Deere #310E is routing out
a stream of asphalt from Hertford
to Queens Road West, the length of our street.
Its clumsy claw digs deep—a modern
Triceratops—voracious in its brutal chewing.

A rusty truck makes a U-turn
on my neighbor's plot of fescue
across his flagstone walk.
He won't like this.
We don't like this interruption,
this cracking of our common spaces
between our point-3 acre claims, exposing
indelicate dirt. The driver with the yellow braid
utters slow commands to his Mexican helper:
Shovel   Broom   Turn   the   truck

Did we do this once to the dirt dwellers,
speak slowly as gods?
This   will   be   good   for   you
These square brick houses. Boundary
fences cut fresh from old-growth cedar.
The river turned inward and tamed.

Laundromat

Back east from the Rockies, I'm passing
wash-time in thick pasty air, settled
in a plastic chair, reading a poem about a man
preaching to a piece of chalk. His recitation
matches the rhythm in this place: muffled beat
of radio oldies, spin cycle, drone
of a commercial fan, every now and then
the staccato slap of my hiking boot on a dryer's
glass door, despite the sign *no shoes in the dryer.*

The poet shifts from sidewalk stranger
to his own dead father, then back to
the street-wise ramble on feldspar, calcium
and oyster shells—all that came before the chalk.
I think about the mountain we climbed
out west, how it was before tectonic plates
cracked open the earth, broke it
into talus and boulder. At its peak,
we scouted storm clouds forming, prelude
to lightning bolts, then re-tracked the rocky trail,

down to the tree line of wild columbine
and lodgepole pines. Vast welcome
of evergreen and not-so-welcome smudges
of brown—pine bark beetles and blue fungus
taking acres. In my woe for the pines,
I'm told what will come instead—more
red-headed woodpeckers, yellow aspens,
a new forest we can only dream.
Talk turned to dinosaurs and polar bears,

the warp and weft of what we know: here
in this laundromat—dust from my boots,
sweaty socks and bedbugs
gathered in creases from a seedy hotel
in a worn-out town at the trail head. Long gone

the lure of gold and silver in that hollow.
Prospectors, outlaws hunkered in brothels,
miners on mule back hauling picks and shovels,
all of them there for a brief breath of time,
sifting and re-sifting the dirt.

Rush Hour

It's hard to tell, from here
on my porch, the species of bird
perched high on a single bare branch
of the tallest oak across the street.

Cardinal. Or common starling.
I like to imagine a red-tailed hawk
and the roar of rush hour
the Gauley River after a winter thaw.

In a minute he'll swoop down
into a granite gorge
for a ritual breakfast
of rabbit or snake.

I *can* do this, can't I—will the city
into woods, dream speed bumps
into boulder hills, fancy English ivy
into tangles of wild blueberries,

paint my grass
with a musty smell of skunk.
And what about the barred owl
hooting outside my window each night?

Can I suppose that he (so dazzled
by house and street lights) thinks
he has somehow lifted into
wilderness sky, settled among stars?

Copal Grill Bulldozed in 67 Minutes

There is no silence like the silence
of dust and rubble on a city street when a city
turns to glitter and glow.

All its old beauties have come down.
Hotels, coliseum, this local diner
that for six decades fed

the working class and out-of-work.
And last year another one, the Coffee Cup,
where black and white sat side by side, even as

the paint was drying on the *Colored*
bathroom door. Gone
are the fish bones, chicken

necks, a past tinged in toil and gristle.
Like a divorce, when a man leaves the house,
takes off with nothing

but his grandfather's silver,
and even that he'd sell for a new iPhone
or carbon frame road bike.

Who needs him anyway?
He's a condo where lush woods used to be, built
on the backs of birds and foxes. Not a bona fide

bungalow left in this town or a greasy spoon
where renegades can perch in suits or overalls,
elbows-to-elbows on the counter.

Grizzled Old Man, a Study

in memory

Early October. A man enters a coffee shop.
Shuffles in from the sidewalk clutching
a tabloid and wadded grocery bag.
     Wrapped in a drab coat and frayed
     woolen hat, I note, too soon in the fall for such

armor of burnish and brown. He bumps
by the case of croissants and fat-free
muffins—*a prickly beard among the clean shaven,*
cowboy coffee in a world of cappuccinos.
     He could be anybody. He could be anybody's

father, mine for one, a long way from little league
and a son who played shortstop. A son gone
to vegetables, the old man to drink.
     Wha'da ya mean, ya don't eat turkey?
he'd caw again this holiday. But he died in June.

At the back of the shop, the man fills his bag
with day-old donuts, turns for the door, walks out
     the way he came, past the hollow buzz
of an espresso machine, a young man
flipping pages of *The New York Times,* stirring his cup.

Geraniums, Blood Red

When my father-in-law speaks of his dead wife
who killed herself at forty-two, he'll tell you
she was *concerned.* My own mother
got a bad case of *nerves,* my aunt
a *malignancy,* and anybody who died back then
simply went to sleep, went to be with their Lord,
went to a better place, unspeakable.

How could we learn to trust
                a pot of *Pelargoniums?*

At eighty, Cousin Eddie had a stroke and
for two years trilled out *Goddamn Jesus Christ*
like a mantra, as if no-*what the hell*-body ever let him
you look nice dear in your double-knit pantsuit
say what was on his *I believe in God the Father* tongue,
so twisted the words had become there
among the sweet and bitter buds.

Buttonholes

At a family gathering, the grandmother fumbles
with her buttons, pearl simulations,
slippery enough to push through

the holes with every flinch and gesture.
It keeps her fingers busy, eyes down
instead of on the grandfather.

Lately she's gone off on him,
hitting, shoving, like corn in a pot of hot grease

or an ant up a pants leg that waits to bite
where flesh is tender and sweet. No matter
the shock treatments or interventions

by their grown children. She's the second wife
in his ninety years, the first one dead at forty-two,

and this one might have been his deliverance
if he had not lived so long. All night
we steer the conversation, trying to keep

that dog on its tether, drowsy in the sun.
But every now and then,
when light moves to shadow,

the brute breaks its chain—her hands
fisted toward the gentle man

then back to the gape at her breast,
fixing what will only come undone.

Seven Pumpkins on a Marquee

I love the way the pumpkins
on the Epworth United Methodist Church marquee
are arranged in descending order of size.
Someone in the congregation must have done this,
a committee member or the preacher's secretary.

For now as I drive past, I'll guess it's the secretary,
a woman who believes in order.
Every morning she makes her bed and
once a week recites the creeds as the men
of 300 A.D. wrote them to be recited,

steadfast and absolute. Likely her father,
a righteous man, told her bedtime stories
of walking to school in snow, scabs on his knees
from digging raw turnips. Maybe she grew
to expect his dollars for As. Why else

would she turn the smooth orange skins
toward traffic. And what will happen in a few days
when Halloween brings out the devils—
the pumpkin smashers. I can imagine her
early on All Saints Day, sweeping up

all evidence of evil. What I'm wishing
in that still dark moment before dawn
is one overlooked fruit—
and her steadfast and absolute will
to rare back and dropkick it into the street.

Girl with Father

after an AP photograph
of an Afghan refugee camp

for Idema

She is crater-eyed, swallowed up with fever
and thirst. Her father can feel death inside her.

The stick of her arm droops from his shoulder,
dropping then a thin green bracelet on dry dirt.

Outside my window, summer's still-green grass
eyes me through fallen leaves, holds on.

Yesterday I raked twenty plump bags full,
left them at the curb for pick-up.

When I was four, my father would pick me up
and flip me inside out until I died with laughter.

He gave me a rake bowed with green satin my first
trip home from college. My birthday comes in the fall.

Her ghost will come soon, leaving him inside out.
All he knows is to swallow the dry sand and hold on.

What Patsy Remembers about Her Father
at Myrtle Beach, 1955

It wasn't so much the way
he took the other girl's hand that summer day
and led her into the ocean,
lifted her over waves and later that night

from his shoulders onto the merry-
go-round. It wasn't so much
the shock on people's faces
to see a *colored* girl
(their family maid's eight-year-old daughter)

on a whites-only
beach and gilded horse.

What it was
was her father's face as he stood there,
hard as a piling in sand, and then
on the boardwalk. Cold stone,
that face, dull and hollow
as the sound of fog on a February sea,
as if he knew his bold gestures
would not make the world right.

Not for the staring strangers.
Not for his own children, busy
in their own bliss, or their mother
staring at stars. Not for the little girl
yelling *Hey Mister Jack,*
on every turn, a*gain, again!*

Shirley Chisholm for President

We've come to Q&A
after a documentary about that fiery spirit
from Brooklyn, first black woman in Congress,
first black, first woman to run for president.
A man in an orange shirt is rising
with the stage lights, telling us (not once
but twice) that he dined with Ms. Chisholm,
though he calls her Shirley.
As if this single kudo is crucial
to his atonement, accountability,
a bridge to brandish his current crown—
PR Deputy of the town's new NBA team, he says,
by now his chest puffed out,
bobcat insignia blazing like an evangel.

Thirty-five years ago
and he's still all prickles and glow,
eight elections later, her candidacy long gone.
I think about more recent candidates
dragging up a worn-out war, battering
medallions about, riding secondhand swift boats
and excuses like stallions.
Maybe Mr. Warhol was right
about our fifteen minutes, that pugnacious bliss
we return to—how at my fiftieth birthday party
I twirled a high school baton, sang every word
of *Shine for Dear Ol' Reynolds*—
how even our heroine at eighty
might still watch old news clips, proof
that no matter what becomes of her,
there was a time when she had it going on.

Winter Solstice, after the Flood

*a tribute to Princeville, North Carolina,
first U.S. town incorporated by freed slaves
(after Hurricane Floyd, September 1999)*

Seems like a long time since you
came by boat to pick their cotton,
virgin white, then planted
your own seeds sometime later
in a lesser place on this meager dirt,
last of the pickings, deeper
than the river. Dirt black as flesh,
black as the night of your first crossing,
black as moldy wood marinating
in the hold, black as the ocean.

You never forgot the ocean or
your rusty chains, and when the rain
turned the river into a sea, stretched it
across decades of fields, repossessed
your anchors, swallowed your doors
and windowsills, you could smell
the hard metal through the stench
of new mold that would come. Again

you were taken on boats, leaving
only watermarks on hollow boards, marks
like the ones that would measure
your children. Again you followed
someone else's star, left this place dark
for the longest night of the year with only
a yellow moon hanging and
a town hall tree pulsing with tiny lights.

I Am Watching the Murder of Ants

My critique group didn't like the poem,
said it was earnest for verse.
                    Just to please,
I took out the word *murder* and the parts
about pinning butterflies to Walmart poster board
and ripping geese (mated for life) from the sky.
Show don't tell, they said, though
Bambi in the freezer would have to go.
          So I promised to show
what I saw that Saturday morning
on the sidelines of the soccer game:
two darling boys, six and three, beating out rhythms
with sticks on an anthill (*little Neanderthals*).
          There I go again,
moralizing their grisly ritual, as natural
to them as steam off hot rocks after rain.
          Show it, I say,
show how they circled the mound of dirt,
pounded it flat, clapped in victory as their parents
clapped for the goal, as surviving ants scattered,
how nobody noticed the difference,
the way some Saturday in spring
          (Sorry, critique group)
when no one's paying attention, whole civilizations
might just up and disappear.

"The Coast of Death"

a found poem, altered, from Mar Roman of AP

In Galicia, they say, all they have is the sea.
Here where people stand before dawn
knee-deep in frigid water, harvesting clams
and cockles for all of Spain and Portugal.

Today its shoreline of craggy coves, thundering
with gray-green waves and shipwrecks (thus
the grim name), is coated in gooey fuel oil
drained from an aging tanker

as it breaks apart and sinks.
A man from Caion, crab and squid catcher,
brushes greasy stains from the plank-front
of his mother-in-law's house.

I used to be a fisherman,
my future now as black as this oil. He speaks
of the dangerous waves he would die to dodge,
if not for that split steel hull, to reach the rocks,

to cut off the goose barnacle, a black
finger-shaped delicacy he'd sell for a fortune,
for someone to steam and snap in two,
suck out its pink, gelatinous flesh.

Memorial Day, Provincetown

Midday at low tide,
and I can't help counting the boats
beached on seaweed and dry sand
among stacks of lobster traps
and orange buoys. A dozen in all,
last summer's abandoned fleet.

Catamarans, whalers, mostly unnamed.
One bares a rough *e-s,* half a *c,* half an *a, p,*
sun-worn remnants of someone's disillusion.

But this is not about the boats.
This is about the man who tends the boats.
Like a frayed gull, he lumbers across the cove
in waders and ragged quills. He leans
into the rusty hull of a 20-footer,
chips a barnacle or loose piece of fiberglass.

His long gray braid falls limp
onto bent shoulders.
If not for this, then what would he be—

yachtsman, tug-boat pilot, naval architect?
Behind us, along the glitzy street,
square-shouldered peacocks
are beginning to strut their tight bodies,
greased and puffed up as fritters.
The old salt drags a dinghy into the sea,

paddles out 50 feet, sets a mooring.
The sky broods gray, as if trying
to keep summer from coming.

Wreck

Like spun sugar they whirled,
whipping up cotton air into

pinks and blues, stone-blind
to the void where stars used to be.

Just for tonight, this one last time,
youth would whisper its lie.

Then it would spin them harder,
watch all but one

cling to something new and odd
and each other, their hands raw clay,

reaching like grails to catch the rain.
But no one can catch rain

this salty, all the night's sweetness wasting
down into a shadowed sluice

beneath the place where only minutes ago
they had danced.

III

The world of dew is the world of dew,
        And yet
        And yet

—*Issa*

Here Nor There

I'm nowhere this morning, though you'll swear
you saw me at this neighborhood diner,
Eddie's Place, ordering three buttermilk pancakes
with melted butter and maple syrup.
After a twelve-hour fast for a cholesterol test,
you'll hear me say *I deserve it.* And besides,
it's raining cold and hard outside
on the greenhouse glass that shelters my booth.
At the bar a TV muffles out
a snow report for the northern counties.

None of this would be a problem, except today
is the first day of spring, and you know how fragile
the cherry blossoms are and this unnamed tree
above my head that's just starting to put out fruit.
I'm just starting to read a travel magazine
I took from the doctor's office
when I lose my sense of place and find I'm
neither here nor there.

Not here at this table with my butter,
plastic salt shaker and two bottles of Tabasco,
nor there, on Parrot Cay in the salty Turks and Caicos,
smothered in a mango-butter facial
or an allspice essential-oil wrap
at a place called *Shambhala,* Sanskrit for utopia,
with a former monk-turned-masseuse named Song,
his trick a mind-altering Indian head massage,
and I'm with him in bougainvillea-ville,
sipping ginger-honey tea instead of decaf
from an Italian ceramic cup. And everywhere

there is water—warm blue ripples on glossy pages,
gray rivulets freezing on this window—so much water
under me, over me, running through me,
that I think I could float right on out of here.

Oldest Town in the Oldest State

On a solo road trip up the coast, I've stopped
to walk these streets. Early scattering
of birch leaves fallen on the sidewalk.

The historical society, barn-red,
leaning on its foundation. Everything else
is as it was—and for a minute

I'm living seaside
in the gambrel-roofed house
with Joshua Fisher, son of a wealthy merchant

who every night sits by candlelight
charting the Delaware Bay while I tend the fire,
or maybe the children, if I happen instead to have

married Ryves Holt, handsome naval officer
of the Port, settled in that shingled cottage on 2nd
and Mulberry where after supper

we'll be found snuggled in homespun wool.
How persistent these romantic notions
I still tote in my satchel. Forty years past college

when I was the lucky one who'd soon
be hanging clothes out to dry. The girls we pitied
were the vagabonds

ambling off to Boston, San Francisco
or, for that matter, Lewes, Delaware, living uncoupled
down the street from Mrs. Holt or Mrs. Fisher.

For better or worse, today I'm that vagabond,
stopping in a lonely town to stroll
a labyrinth in an ancient churchyard

and read brass plaques of those who led
the life expected. In an hour I'll catch
a ferry to Cape May, dig my toes in sand

along the shore, gather images and words
for my own marker—a feminine rhyme or two,
a ballade in blank verse.

Clichéd

It's hard to recapture
what we felt when you told the realtor
we were tickled pink
over the old house.
That seaport city, honeyed
in old houses, and now this one, ours.
Yes, we were giddy about it.
Yet it wouldn't be long
before you'd pull up
another common jingle:
I just don't hear the bells anymore.
That said, we'd put it away,
keep ripping walls to bare bones,
scraping and sanding
heart pine floors, stripping
decades of paint from plaster, making
our first child. Look at her—
thirty-one and undeniably
the apple of our eyes, love of our life.
There's no overusing those words.
And what about *conceived in love.*
Something grander
than wide yellow planks
and banistered porches, close enough
to the harbor for us to smell salt air
on damp days, hear a tugboat
blow warnings of an incoming barge.

Brief History of Trees

They're taking it down—
my neighbor's willow oak that was struck
last summer. I thought it might survive,

but lightning's white heat sliced deep,
gashing a channel from earth
to sky. A heart-line.

For too many years, I've lived under
the loom and sway of these trees.
Bones breaking in the ice of '03.
Hurricane of '89 that sent us

to inner rooms where my then-husband
and I huddled with our small daughters.
Outside, dark limbs cracked and popped.

Inside, storms already between us.
A wet wind spewed.
Now and then, a hollow thud.

I've cursed the trees, dreamed of living
in a desert or on the coast.
Yet there's a tug for this one—the X
painted on its trunk, bright orange band

flagging surrender, leafy branches
slashed to naked stubs,
that ugly inconsolable scar.

Spell for an Old Boyfriend

Because I walked in the park today
lapping the lake with heat from an overdue autumn
burning inside me

Because I lapped the lake today burning
and the wet air was licking the skin on my arms
and leaves were falling like feathers

Because the air was wet and the leaves falling
and wild geese were flying south on a shaft
of hot white light

Because the geese flying south
made a mockery of my resolve
and you were everywhere in the park today

Because you were all over me in the park
but especially in the guise of the lead goose
vanishing like vapor into blue sky

Because you could vanish so deftly like a bird
and especially because in the middle of the lake
there was this lone white goose

raging low and lonely and
because I can turn the metaphor on a whim
today I'll make you the lone white goose

Back Road in Tuscany, a Morning Walk

What about these Buddhist prayer flags,
        Signore Staccioli,
adorning the iron gate of the villa
that bears your name? I have the same ones
back home, draped around a garden-shed post.

They're tattered and faded like yours.

Would our souls be mates if you invited me
for cappuccino and an almond biscotti,
if languages could meld and I left my tour,
canceled the newspaper,
sent for my cats,

all for a life of slow food and sangiovese?

The sun is just beginning to burn
the mist from your olive trees, and from over
the hill, an echo of a hunter's gun—someone
out for wild boar, I'm told.

Dear prayer flags—bless and protect me
from the wild boar,
                the sting of gunshot,
this season of harvest and heat,
        the next man who asks me in.

Preparing for a Daughter's Move West

for Caroline

The deer have come early to feed—first
a young buck with his mother, then
six more does and a fawn. They've gathered

next to a gravel driveway under dogwoods
and red maple that only hours ago were bathed
by a slanted moon. From a window frame,

I watch them bend their necks toward
a mound of corn, lift and nibble, bend again.
One stands apart, chewing her cud.

She is so close I can see each muscle
flex and swell from stomach to throat. I watch
every swallow she makes, every twitch

of her veined ears, alert to the unexpected.
Back in the herd, the fawn moves in to suckle.
Its mother nudges it away from the others,

out of my sight to a place I know I can't go.
Still, I press my cheek against the glass
to peer past blue salvia and cleome,

a loose stack of broken limbs
at the woods' edge and, beyond that,
flickers of light and dark through the trees.

Cat Lost in a Storm

Now that the rain and wind have stalled,
　　　the gaping door again latched,
what may work is for all of us

to go outside and breathe into the air
　　　for thirty seconds or so, the words
come home Woody, come home Woody,
come home, all the while

envisioning that gray tabby creeping down
　　　the trunk of a large tree or lifting
himself from under a porch stoop
where he's tucked himself away

from chaos. Not that I'm
　　　a Pollyanna, but there's got to be
something to the notion that a flutter

of Brazilian butterfly wings can activate
　　　tornadoes in Texas, a tiny circumstance
that just may change one's course—

for the Canada goose on her nest
at the greenway last week, if only someone
　　　had chanted *go away snapping turtle,*
go away, but especially for Woody

because my daughter named him
　　　after that great songwriter
who could turn hearts inside out with his
Talking Blues or *I Ain't Got No Home,*

and if he could do that, don't you think
　　　with a sweet meditation or two,
we could coax our little cat back.

Because It Crumbled
in an Unnamed Storm of '62

my mother and aunts still pace
like sentries along the breezeway, marking
off the night, while under pilings, we girls
hold fort in sleeping bags and damp dreams.
The men have taken their highballs to bed.

A rusty chain on the porch swing sings
its repetitious riddle. Dogs long gone
of bone and sinew bark and race the surf
for seagulls, steady as a church creed.

In a wooden shower,
warm pee puddles at the feet
of small brown bodies eager for sleep.

Our barren aunt bakes us sand biscuits
light as morning, sneaks us sodas
for supper, lets us wrap her in miles of gauze
like a mummy. She and the mothers
are gone now, and the fathers,

and every board and shingle, and
because in the mingle of shattered glass
the only reclamation was the icebox
stocked with bluefish, fresh-caught
and still cool to touch, and because

I will never go back,
I'll forever be twelve and tender.

No one will grow old there or bent with time.
Lap pools at low tide will hold whole worlds.
The women will shelter, their voices soft
as attic dust. And somewhere
in some ocean, for the men's sake,
the blues will always be running.

Pilgrim's Highway, a Meditation

It must be more than whimsy,
the name of this road I'm crossing
between Boston and Cape Cod.
I've traveled here to stretch my edges,
explore this *terra firma* before it becomes

a disequilibrium of small sandy planets.
Some people spend their whole lives
counting windowpanes. My father
always said *we'll move to the coast,*
but his fishing poles grew moldy

in the dim corner of our pine-paneled den.
His mother's place in the country
had been gone forty years, yet the earth
was still there, its red clay
too raw to unstick his rooted boots.

Five miles to Sagamore Bridge
and an island named for a fish I've never
heard of. In the curve to my right,
someone has painted a cinderblock house
the color of lime sherbet—who

knows why. Everywhere
summer growth is starting to bud,
and this I know: before it blooms full,
the land I'm driving on
is bound to give way to the sea.

Elements

The finest workers in stone are not copper or steel tools but
the gentle touches of air and water working at their leisure
with a liberal allowance of time.
                                                    —Henry David Thoreau

Somewhere there's a grown man whose father has died,
a man who is riffling through a dresser drawer
and finds the start of a note, *Dear son, don't know...*

and because the note is dated *Sat. Oct. 10, '98* and penned
on a glossy postcard with a picture of red rock arching into blue sky,
he figures it's a thank you for their trip out west that year.

On the card is a quote about time. The man thinks about time
and wonders why his father's words had stopped short—a call
to the supper table, distraction on TV,

or simply a tongue struck dumb by the unspeakable
touches on the photograph of air and water, shadow and light.
It was always the elements that connected

the two of them—fall's camouflage, crack of winter footsteps
in the woods, even last summer's blaze that scorched
so many trees they had once named.

The man holds the unfinished note in his hand, and because
he is one who saves everything, he will save it, reading
over and over what lingers there between rock and sky.

A Man Buries His Dog

The way he tells it, lightning
was carving the sky into threads—a late

afternoon rumble he knew would send
his fourteen-year-old Sal bolting.

Grinding out that last twist of country road,
he got there too late, another car before him,

its driver pacing the shoulder, stooping, pacing.
At the road's edge he saw her, and

for a moment neither sad nor mad,
he slipped into her skin, her familiar

brindled fur, felt the raw hot asphalt
on his back. Then he was back,

lifting her, carrying her home,
digging a place in his wife's perennials.

All the while, that fickle sky, he says,
sputtered, hissed, spit down on him,

spilled nothing—not even a cup of water
to soften the thirsty dirt beneath his shovel.

Knowing the Odds for Snowfall in the South

Even so, I watch in my small backyard
as, all at once, thirty birds

drop hard out of a white sky
to swallow dry my birdbath and dog's dish,

the rainy remnants from an old clay pot.
Wing to wing, they bow and dip

their beaks—rounds of robins, their mussed
and ruffled breasts glowing like hot coals,

gold finches poised in fitted suits,
a cardinal couple, some middling wrens.

Suddenly they lift, press into a south wind.
As they go, the sky

begins to shatter as if
they are pulling it down behind them

on invisible strings, shards of glass and glitter
filling the empty vessels indubitably.

Once I Saw a Frozen Waterfall

She was clutching a granite wall
in that January hush, as if to keep
      each rock
from falling into the river below.

      Silver braids
criss-crossed her back.
Her robe was glittered in jewels, raw
diamonds that seemed to be

strung mid-air like gasps
      of breath—or fists.
Only a woman bereft of flow
would hold in her hands

      all the year's watershed:
tears of dew, unsettled rain,
fog that may never warm to vapor.
Only she, on that winter day,

or any day, would pause
to gather her spumescence,
      daring the sun
that angles through forest bones

to melt even one drop
of all she claims, all
that in the spring (when she is ready)
      will set her free.

Naming the White Mare

She'll have none of our ritual, this
dew-eyed Andalusian who was brought
to the sanctuary last week,
starved and broken. We whisper
Treasure   Rain   Shenandoah
Belezia   Winter

as we watch for a sign—a vigorous nod,
some licking and chewing, ears
pricked toward our voices.

It's custom to re-name the horses
when they come here, but this new girl
is tougher than most. No quiver
of skin we might take as concession,

she seems slow to cloak herself
with humanspeak—one more come-on
of sweet syllables, another siren song
that could lead her anywhere—
a mucked-up stall, a pitted field.

One of us wants to try *Shalimar* next.
Another, who's had her share of losses,
suggests we ask the horse to tell us
her name. We gently touch her neck,
her withers, listen and wait, hold still
as a pasture in full bloom.

Surgery

And so I'm being rolled down
a dark hall toward a place of light
to have my breasts reduced
for some reason I can't quite understand,
being one who, in lessons of geography,
was always foothills if not sea level. Over me

the doctor is in shadow, maybe bearded.
He gives me diagrams and then a shot.
By now we're on the interstate
at early rush hour and, though befuddled,
I'm conscious of signs
for exit ramps looming above me.

With a voice that could have come only
from a dream, I say *stop,* and he does,
though he's not pleased.
New orders, plain-spoken: *Return*
to prep, douse yourself in water
until you wake. He releases me

to my fifteen-year-old daughter who
re-weaves us through traffic like a master.
Still prone, I gaze at the back
of her head to see the loveliest sight—
flickers of sunlight and spiders
in her hair, spinning all that gold into braids.

Rest Home Rollers

Those who can are out for a little creep,
zigging and zagging hallways,
clumped lumpy in wheelchairs like laundry

or bags of sand. Daughters
of the American Revolution, Junior League
presidents from Huntsville, Alabama

or Cincinnati, deacon of the First Presbyterian Church
in Columbus, Georgia, a teacher from the Bronx.

Nurses, masters of cello or hand stitch,
master gardeners, master rabble-rousers,
a closet lesbian or two, a poet with an ax to grind.

Limbs knotted in tangles of twist and bend,
boulders lading their backs, it's a virtual boneyard
here where they've come to linger. Yet

they'll scoot all day, these diapered divas,
wherever somewhere or nowhere calls.

Meet Mildred from Bayfield, Wisconsin
on a go-cart with an older sister, Sally, spring of '26.

Or Liddybet taxiing the runway
in a yellow Piper Cub, her first solo. She'll swear

it's the forties in Kalamazoo after the war.
And over there by the gas pump, arm draped
out a Studebaker window, her high school beau

still telling his same old joke. He's part of the pack
that fills the halls today, come to deliver the gals
from sag and bone and hammertoes.

The wheels of the bus go round and round,
sings Pinkie to her pillow. *Are you my daughter?*
she asks, while Pat revs her bumper car

on a hot Coney Island boardwalk with a carny-hunk
named Ricky, his hand on her thigh.

Rear View

You pull over to the shoulder
of a split two-lane and consider
the possibilities. Something has made you stop.
The strip-worn storefronts, maybe, a faded
blue-green awning over what used to be
the town's feed and hardware? Or was it

remnants of that antique pipe dream called
Casablanca? Next door, a *For Sale* sign curls
in the glare of a Thrift Market window. Who
would buy a thrift market in this withered place?
No matter. Something made you loop back
under an old railroad trestle at the junction

of Florida State 24 and US 301. How familiar
these live oaks, their gray limbs weighted with
Spanish moss, reminding you it's winter.
You've been here in winter. And if you see
a rusted caboose tethered to an empty
playground, you'll recall some story your father

told about a turn-of-the-century passenger train
running north to south, an opera house. For you,
it was the way to Grandmother's, before
the road gave way to I-95, sucking the life
out of this town named Waldo. Let's say today
you amble up the road to the Classic Inn Motel,

a horseshoe of twenty-four dingy rooms, dirt
where a pool used to be. If you look hard you'll see
a '58 two-tone blue Buick parked out front,
a mother walking a little brown dog in the grass,
two children racing to get into bathing suits,
a father paying the clerk $13 for the night

and unpacking a small brown paper bag. You'd like
a drink about now, a glass of pinot grigio
or cold beer. But you're miles from home.
You glance once more at the old red caboose,
consider the feel of wheel on track,
check your mirror before pulling out.

After Restoration

From the 1900s to the 1960s, Glen Echo was a premier amusement park in the Washington, DC area. Its crowning jewel was the Dentzel carousel installed in 1921.

The band organ plays a goodnight waltz
as I hand my ticket to the man.
A bell clangs its brass warning.
My palomino rises and falls.

I hand my ticket to the man.
What gravity this rebirth of color,
my palomino rising and falling,
bridled in emeralds and gold.

What gravity this rebirth of color
from the 1920s, end of a trolley line,
bridled in emeralds and gold,
making steady circles of sound and color.

The 1920s, end of a trolley line.
Is that my father on the appaloosa,
making steady circles of sound and color?
He used to come here.

Is that my father on the appaloosa
circling my same platform?
He used to come here.
How twisted this thing called time.

Circling my same platform
our horses begin to mellow.
How twisted this thing called time,
no beginning, no end.

Our horses begin to mellow,
the motion slows.

No beginning, no end,
just a gradual gripping of the brake.

The motion slows.
A bell clangs its brass warning.
With a gradual gripping of the brake,
the band organ plays a goodnight waltz.

On Easter Sunday, I Opt
for Sunrise on a Cottage Porch

All I wanted was to watch the sky crack
(old terracotta sky-shell), watch it set free its mysterious

yolk. Just another day, some would say—life

a series of days stacked like plates, waiting
for some feast to be served.

But on this day
in this unsteepled place, I catch new light

as it breaks, and—surprising the beach—find

(even as dark is lifting) sea oaks awake, swaying
to the steady pulse of ocean's beat,

and little signs
that, all night, sand crabs were busy

criss-crossing the dunes, leaving them empty
for us to wonder about in the morning.

I've Chased the Sun across Ten States

to break strings I can't even name.
So when a stranger tells me
You gotta see Child's Glacier, take my truck,
I drive out the only road in town.

Town that's a bar and tuna cannery,
everywhere the smell of fish sludge stirred
by greedy gulls. Unpolished cove
called Cordova, all that's left
of a mining boom. Old Alaska.

Locals say when they painted the old hotel,
they re-tacked the sign upside down
like it had always been. People
stubborn as hemlocks.

And here I plod, untamed grip
on the wheel—100 miles full-loop
on a cryptic strip of rust and rubble,
barely clearing the Copper River.
I didn't think I could stand a place

this lonely. No choice but to go all the way
where the earthquake of '64
broke up the bridge, dead-ended
the road, making this the end of the world.

Last year the glacier dropped a chunk
of herself into the river, spurring a deadly
tidal wave. Yet folks keep coming out
to hear her calving, see the show.
It's what I've come to do—step out

of this truck, ease toward
the water's edge, fix my eyes
on the slick of her blue-green skin,
listen for the terrible cracking of bones.

Watching Death

Here on the cold abandoned
volcanic crust of Haleakala, *house of the sun,*
there's only porous ash and earth's hostility.
      Yet ten thousand feet above
hibiscus, kona snow flowers, bougainvillea,
an odd plant burns like a taper.
      'Ahinahina. Silversword.

Clumps of it glitter in the pre-dawn light,
its soft gray hairs curving inward
to shield it from heat and draft.
      Understated, but at some random moment
in fifty years (science can't explain the order)
each will spike a purple bloom—then die.

Today one has flowered.
Who of us can say why this one,
on this day, or when the next?
I turn to the sunrise—something I can count on.
      A long thin purple line begins to flame.

Pu-rog-atory

for Joe Rob

Santa Margherita, preserved for centuries
at the altar of this Tuscan church,
looks good for her age. *Seven hundred*

is the new three hundred, our guide quips
as we ogle that tiny corpse
through glass, lapis and gold.

Soon I'll be sixty, dread
every wrinkle and sag—too vain
for sainthood in a glass casket.

She straddles two worlds. In death,
she's a thousand blue stones above
the Via Nationale with its Sunday strollers

in tight jeans and leather boots.
In life she bore a cross for the poor
and hungry. Like the homeless man

who showed me a piece of his art,
a gathering of faceless heads
carved on a pine scrap.

Judgment Day, he explained, *you know,*
like Pu-rog-atory. Call it what you like,
Mr. Joe—limbo, space between

birthdays, grace between saint
and forsaken—we are all, real or unreal,
ghosts of flesh and bone.

Acknowledgments

Grateful acknowledgment to the editors of the following journals and anthologies in which these poems, sometimes in an earlier version, originally appeared:

Aurorian: "Past Curfew"
Charlotte Viewpoint: "The Unblooming," "Wild Plums"
Charlotte Writers Club Anthology: "Paperwhites"
Icarus: "Bulldozer," "Because It Crumbled in an Unnamed Storm of '62"
    (Honorable Mention)
Iodine: "Rest Home Rollers"
Kakalak Anthology: "Here Nor There," "Snorkling the Big Island"
    (Honorable Mention)
...and love Anthology: "Elements"
Main Street Rag: "What Patsy Remembers about her Father at Myrtle
    Beach, 1955," "A Starving Musician Takes a Church Job," "Rear View"
Queens University Margaret Blankenship Prize: "Winter Solstice"
Southern Women's Review: "Bodegónes"
The Sow's Ear Poetry Review: "Pu-rog-atory"
Tar River Poetry: "Re-Vamped," "Cat Lost in a Storm"
Wild Goose Poetry Review: "On Buying a Writing Desk after the Death of
    My Daughter's Best Friend"

The following poems were also included in the chapbook, *The Gravity of Color,* published by Main Street Rag: "Tinted Snapshots Under Glass," "Halftones," "Re-Vamped," "Sweet," "Because It Crumbled in an Unnamed Storm of '62," and "After Restoration."

I am deeply grateful to my poetry group—Rebecca McClanahan, Gail Peck, Diana Pinckney, Barbara Presnell, Dede Wilson, and Terri Wolfe—for all they did to help make this book a reality; for their time, their talent, and their friendship.

Cover art, "Pigeons Flight," by Patryk Specjal; author photo by Katy Cobb; cover and interior book design by Diane Kistner (dkistner@futurecycle.org); interior text and titling, Adobe Garamond Pro

About FutureCycle Press

FutureCycle Press is dedicated to publishing lasting English-language poetry and flash fiction books, chapbooks, and anthologies in both print-on-demand and ebook formats. Founded in 2007 by long-time independent editor/publishers and partners Diane Kistner and Robert S. King, the press incorporated as a nonprofit in 2012. A number of our editors are distinguished poets and authors in their own right, and we have been actively involved in the small press movement going back to the early seventies.

The FutureCycle Poetry Book Prize and honorarium is awarded annually for the best full-length volume of poetry we publish in a calendar year. We are dedicated to giving all authors we publish the care their work deserves, making our catalog of titles the most distinguished it can be, and paying forward any earnings to fund more great books.

We've learned a few things about independent publishing over the years. We've also evolved a unique, resilient publishing model that allows us to focus mainly on vetting and preserving for posterity the most books of exceptional quality without becoming overwhelmed with bookkeeping and mailing, fundraising activities, or taxing editorial and production "bubbles." To find out more about what we are doing, come see us at www.futurecycle.org.

The FutureCycle Poetry Book Prize

All full-length volumes of poetry published by FutureCycle Press in a given calendar year are considered for the annual FutureCycle Poetry Book Prize. This allows us to consider each submission on its own merits, outside of the context of a contest. Too, the judges see the finished book, which will have benefitted from the beautiful book design and strong editorial gloss we are famous for.

The book ranked the best in judging is announced as the prize-winner in the subsequent year. There is no fixed monetary award; instead, the winning poet receives an honorarium of 20% of our total net royalties from all poetry books and chapbooks we sold online that year. (For example, in 2013, the winner of the 2012 book prize was announced and received a cash award from the 2012 royalties.) The winner is also accorded the honor of serving as a judge in the next year's competition and, as such, receives a copy of all prize contenders' books.